Crime Reduction Research Series Paper 2

Neighbourhood Warden Schemes:

An overview

Jessica Jacobson, Esther Saville

Editor: Barry Webb
Home Office
Policing and Reducing Crime Unit
Research, Development and Statistics Directorate
Clive House, Petty France
London, SW1H 9HD

Policing and Reducing Crime Unit:
Crime Reduction Research Series

RDS
Research Development Statistics

The Policing and Reducing Crime Unit (PRCU) is based in the Research, Development and Statistics (RDS) Directorate of the Home Office. The Unit carries out and commissions social and management science research on policing and crime reduction, to support Home Office aims and develop evidence-based policy and practice.

The Crime Reduction Research Series presents research findings and guidance material relevant to practitioners involved in crime reduction at the local level, and particularly the local crime and disorder partnerships. The series will include work funded under the Government's Crime Reduction Programme as well as other relevant RDS work.

Details of how to obtain further copies of this report can be found on the back cover.

© Crown Copyright 1999   ISBN 1-84082-349-6
First Published 1999

Foreword

The Social Exclusion Unit's report 'Bringing Britain Together' analysed the problems facing the most deprived places in the country. The report highlights neighbourhood wardens as one of the methods proposed by the Government to provide joined-up answers to some of the problems of our poorest neighbourhoods – decaying housing, unemployment, crime, the fear of crime, anti-social behaviour and community break-up. A Policy Action Team was set up to consider this further and to develop proposals.

This present report was undertaken to inform the Policy Action Team's work, by providing an overview of current neighbourhood warden schemes and what is known about their effectiveness. The 50 schemes featured in this report vary enormously in terms of the problems they address, the methods they employ, their scale and funding and the partners involved. While there is a lack of thorough evaluations, the available evidence suggests that warden schemes can help to address many of the problems faced by deprived neighbourhoods. The report identifies the key issues involved in developing and sustaining schemes. As such, it should be of practical value to all agencies working in the community, from Crime and Disorder partnerships and housing authorities to residents' associations and community development workers.

Professor Ken Pease
Acting Head of Policing and Reducing Crime Unit
Research, Development and Statistics Directorate
Home Office
November 1999

Acknowledgements

The current work was undertaken to support the Social Exclusion Unit's Policy Action Team on neighbourhood wardens. We would like to thank the Policy Action Team members for their guidance and expertise in this area which was extremely valuable throughout the research.

We would also like to thank all those involved in organising the visits we made to a number of schemes throughout England and Wales for the helpfulness and hospitality they offered. Visits were conducted to the following schemes: some of the Stadswacht (civic warden) Schemes in the Netherlands, Aylesbury Estate Security Patrol, Swansea Estate Wardens and Neighbourhood Support Unit, Sedgefield Community Force, Hartlepool Central Estate Project, Headrow Housing Group Liason Tennants Scheme, HOPE Halton moor and Osmandthorpe Project for Elders (Leeds), Leeds Federated Housing Association Resident Estate Worker Scheme, Manningham Mutual Aid Project, Middlesborough Council Estate Caretaker Service and Newport Estate Ranger Scheme.

We would also like to thank Ann Deehan (PRC) and Iain Walsh (Secretary of PAT) for their assistance with the development of the project.

The Authors

Jessica Jacobson and Esther Saville are members of the Policing and Reducing Crime Unit.

PRC would like to thank Dr Janet Foster of the Institute of Criminology at the University of Cambridge for acting as an independent assessor for this report.

Executive Summary

Background

The Social Exclusion Unit report Bringing Britain Together (1998) proposed a national strategy for improving the conditions of Britain's poorest neighbourhoods. One element of the proposed strategy is the encouragement of neighbourhood warden schemes. It is suggested that some problems associated with crime and fear of crime can be tackled through the presence of a full-time, recognisable 'warden' with the capacity to take preventive action against crime and disorder and provide general assistance to residents.

The aim of this study was to find out what kinds of neighbourhood warden schemes are currently in existence in Britain and, where possible, to examine the effectiveness of such schemes.

The research

The concept of the 'neighbourhood warden' can be interpreted in a variety of ways. For the purposes of this research, the concept was broadly defined, in order that information could be collected on as wide a range of schemes as possible. Hence 'neighbourhood warden schemes' were understood to be those which encompass each of the following three elements:

- Schemes which cover – in part at least – **residential areas**. These are not restricted to areas of public housing, but include housing association, privately rented and owner-occupied housing.
- The **appointment of individuals** as 'wardens', 'caretakers' or similar by local authorities, private security firms, residents'/tenants' associations, housing associations, multi-agency partnerships, or on a voluntary basis to fulfil certain objectives based upon the specific problems of the area.
- The **functions** of the 'wardens' may include any, or all of the following: security patrols; environmental improvements (including minor repairs, removal of litter and graffiti, planting trees, traffic control); tenant liaison; information provision to residents; information provision to the police and local authority; visits to vulnerable tenants and victims of crime and harassment (including intimidated witnesses); and responding to neighbour disputes and anti-social behaviour.

There were two main components to the research on warden schemes. First, material on a wide range of existing, or recent, schemes across Britain was collected through contacting agencies running schemes and visiting selected sites. The objective was not to produce an exhaustive list of schemes, but to gain information about a wide cross-section, in order to identify the major components of the most common types of scheme. The second element of the research was a review of published literature on warden schemes and related issues.

Findings

Through these means, information was acquired about a total of 50 existing and recent projects, all but one of which are based in Britain. (The exception is the Dutch Stadswacht scheme, included in this study because of its wide-scale use and significant impact across the Netherlands.)

Functions of the schemes

The 50 schemes examined by this study vary widely in terms of their precise objectives, the methods they employ, the size and characteristics of the areas they cover, and their costs, funding and management. Most schemes have several overlapping aims and use various means in seeking to achieve these aims.

However, the most common objectives of the schemes can be summarised in terms of the following three core issues:
- **crime prevention:** that is, reducing levels of crime, anti-social behaviour, and fear of crime;
- **environmental improvements:** including the removal of litter and graffiti, improving the appearance and general state of repair of properties and public areas; and
- **community development:** involving, for example, the promotion of community solidarity and confidence in local agencies, and intolerance of crime and disorder.

The methods most frequently used by the various schemes in pursuing the above three aims, respectively, are as follows:
- **establishment of patrols/concierge schemes:** for example, Southwark Council employs a private security firm to carry out foot patrols on the Aylesbury Estate;
- **employment of caretakers/supercaretakers:** as in the case of a resident estate worker employed by Leeds Federated Housing Association to oversee the day-to-day maintenance of the housing stock and public areas on the estate; and
- **promotion of community organisations:** for example, the residents' association on a Hartlepool estate has appointed a community development worker who has helped to set up youth projects, a new community centre, and a newsletter for residents.

Partnership

Most of the warden schemes reviewed by this research are managed by housing authorities: namely, the housing departments of local authorities and housing associations. However, partnership is a crucial aspect of a large number of the initiatives – with the police, various funding bodies, residents' associations, health and employment services, and specialist housing bodies also being involved in the planning and implementation of many schemes. There is police input into most of the schemes that have security functions, which often includes contributions to the training of personnel. About half of the schemes receive at least partial funding from the local authority; other key sources of funding include housing associations, tenant charges, and the Single Regeneration Budget.

Locations

Neighbourhood warden schemes can operate in a wide range of different contexts. Two-thirds of the schemes examined here are estate-based, but some cover large areas. For example, the Sedgefield Community Force is a council-run force charged with conducting a 24-hour uniformed patrol of the public streets of the entire local authority area. At the other end of the scale, the 'mutual aid' project in Manningham, Bradford, involves the residents of a housing association development of 25 properties.

Impact

This study found that little research has been conducted to date to examine the impact and effectiveness of neighbourhood warden schemes. There is a clear need for thorough evaluations to be carried out, with the aim of establishing which aspects of schemes are having the most beneficial effects, and which aspects may not work as well.

The Home Office Policing and Reducing Crime Unit are commissioning research to fill this gap by conducting thorough evaluations of a small sample of neighbourhood warden schemes. The research will analyse the impact of the schemes on levels of crime and disorder and the quality of life in local areas, assess the cost-effectiveness of schemes, and identify elements of good practice in the planning and implementation of schemes.

The emerging evidence cited in this report – based on the findings of research visits, and the limited monitoring and evaluation exercises that have been carried out – does suggest that warden schemes can help to address many of the problems faced by deprived neighbourhoods. It appears that schemes, often in conjunction with other local crime prevention initiatives, can contribute to bringing down levels of crime and fear of crime. Warden schemes which encompass environmental and community-based aims, perhaps together with crime prevention elements, can help to reverse the social and physical decline of poor areas. In drawing on the skills, expertise and good-will of a variety of local individuals and agencies, many schemes engage in constructive and wide-ranging partnership activities which have tangible impacts upon lives.

Contents

List of case studies

List of figures

List of tables

1.   Introduction

This report presents the findings of a research project initiated to support the work of the Social Exclusion Unit's Policy Action Team on neighbourhood wardens. The aim of the research was to provide an overview of existing knowledge about neighbourhood warden schemes and, where possible, to give indications of effectiveness.

Why study neighbourhood wardens?

The third report of the Social Exclusion Unit, Bringing Britain Together (1998), proposes a national strategy for improving the conditions of Britain's poorest neighbourhoods: those 'pockets of intense deprivation where the problems of unemployment and crime are acute and hopelessly tangled up with poor health, housing and education'.

The encouragement of neighbourhood warden schemes is one element of the proposed national strategy. It is suggested that some problems associated with crime and fear of crime can be tackled through the presence of a full-time, recognisable 'warden' with the capacity to take preventive action against crime and disorder and provide general assistance to residents.

In three respects, the concept of the neighbourhood warden ties in closely with a great deal of current thinking about policies for addressing crime and related problems. First, the concept focuses on local solutions: that is, schemes must be tailored to meet the specific needs of the areas in which they operate, and must involve all relevant agencies working on the ground as well as local people. Secondly, and following from the above, partnership is likely to be an aspect of neighbourhood warden schemes which combine security, housing and environmental goals. Thirdly, the crime prevention dimension to warden schemes reflects the increasing emphasis within policing upon 'proactive', 'problem-solving' approaches to crime.

The importance of these three aspects of neighbourhood warden schemes is reinforced by the Crime and Disorder Act (1998), which specifies that the police, local authorities and other responsible agencies should together produce local audits of crime and disorder, and strategies for tackling these. Some crime and disorder strategies may include provisions for neighbourhood warden schemes, the precise components of which will be determined by the problems identified by the audits. Thus, the strategies provide an opportunity for neighbourhood warden schemes to emerge as an integral element of a wider community safety strategy.

Research methodology

The research proceeded on the basis of a broad definition of 'neighbourhood warden', according to which warden schemes are those which encompass each of the following three elements:

- Schemes which cover – in part at least – **residential areas**. These are not restricted to areas of public housing, but include housing association, privately rented and owner-occupied housing.
- The **appointment of individuals** as 'wardens', 'caretakers' or similar by local authorities, private security firms, residents'/tenants' associations, housing associations, multi-agency partnerships, or on a voluntary basis to fulfil certain objectives based upon the specific problems of the area.
- The **functions** of the 'wardens' may include any or all of the following: security patrols; environmental improvements (including minor repairs, removal of litter and graffiti, planting trees, traffic control); tenant liaison; information provision to residents; information provision to the police and local authority; visits to vulnerable tenants and victims of crime and harassment (including intimidated witnesses); and responding to neighbour disputes and anti-social behaviour.

There were two main components to the research on warden schemes. First, material on a wide range of existing, or recent, schemes across Britain was collected through contacting agencies running schemes and visiting selected sites. The objective was not to produce an exhaustive list of schemes, but to gain information about a wide cross-section, in order to identify the major components of the most common types of scheme. The second element of the research was a review of published literature on warden schemes and related issues.

Through these means, information was acquired about a total of 50 existing and recent projects which fit, or approximate, the definition of 'neighbourhood warden schemes' outlined above. All but one of these schemes are based in the United Kingdom; the exception is the Dutch Stadswacht scheme (Case Study 1), which involves uniformed patrols in public places and is in operation in over 150 municipalities. This scheme is of particular interest because of its wide-scale use across the Netherlands.

The 50 schemes examined by this study vary widely in terms of their objectives, the size and characteristics of the areas they cover, and their costs, funding and management. This variety, and the fact that the material received on projects was very mixed in quality and kind, makes summarising the research findings difficult. Therefore the aim of this paper is not to present general conclusions about effectiveness and aspects of good practice, but rather to outline the main ways in which warden schemes tend to operate, and to consider the issues that must be addressed by those seeking to design, establish or evaluate such projects.

Certain warden schemes are associated with, or have as one component, Neighbourhood Watch.[1] Despite the parallels and links between many neighbourhood warden and Neighbourhood Watch schemes in terms of aims and indeed certain methods, the latter have not been examined by this research since they tend not to entail the introduction of an official or semi-official presence to a local area.

---

[1] Neighbourhood Watch projects – of which there are currently approximately 155,000 in the United Kingdom – are set up with the support of the police, and take the form of community-based crime prevention. Participants in projects may be involved in any of a wide range of activities, depending on the specifics of the crime problems they wish to tackle. Activities may include, for example, informal surveillance, property-marking, home security improvements, and may even extend to organising social events and street cleaning (Laycock and Tilley, 1995).

Structure of the report

The key findings of the research are discussed in the following four chapters. Chapter Two considers the major components of neighbourhood warden schemes; in Chapter Three the discussion then moves on to partnership issues; the fourth chapter examines questions of evaluation; and, finally, Chapter Five presents conclusions. Seven case studies, illustrating various applications of the concept of the neighbourhood warden in England, Wales and the Netherlands, are included in the text.

In Appendix A, an overview of the 50 schemes that have been reviewed is displayed in the form of a table.

CASE STUDY 1: The Stadswacht (Civic Warden) Schemes, the Netherlands

Focus and aims

The civic wardens carry out uniformed patrols in public places. The first scheme was launched in the town of Dordrecht in 1989; today, over 150 (out of a total of about 500) municipalities have operational civic wardens. The rapid growth in the number of schemes resulted in the formation of the Dutch Civic Warden Foundation (Stichting Stadswacht Nederland) in 1992, which is an umbrella organisation for affiliated local schemes. The schemes are managed by local authorities, with some direction from central government and the Foundation.

The schemes have a dual purpose. One aim is to increase feelings of public safety, through the deterrent effect of the uniformed presence on crime and anti-social behaviour. The other aim is to provide job-seekers with the opportunity of acquiring training and work-experience with a view to proceeding to employment outside the scheme.

Staffing and partnership

The tasks of the civic wardens consist of:
● Providing a conspicuous presence and issuing warnings: the preventive function.
● Tackling anti-social behaviour: the corrective function.
● Acting as eyes-and-ears for other agencies: the warning function.
● Acting as host or hostess on behalf of the municipality: the service function.

Wardens do not have special powers, and hence must rely upon persuasion in their dealings with people. They are also responsible for passing on information to the police in the form of daily reports; and incidents going beyond their competence are immediately reported to the police via radio contact.

Civic wardens are recruited and selected from the ranks of the long-term unemployed (individuals who have been unemployed for more than one year). Their wages consist of their regular social security payments topped up with a supplement of 10-20%. The training offered to wardens covers a range of issues, including law, communication, and health and safety.

There was some initial resistance to the warden schemes from the police, but this has now been largely overcome. The activities of the wardens are seen to complement rather than compete with those of the police, and to free up police time for dealing with serious incidents. Relationships with other agencies have been helped by the umbrella Stadswacht organisation, which promotes exchanges on good practice, the accreditation of training, and other matters.

Costs and funding

The costs of the wardens' wages are met by the Department of Employment, and local authorities cover the overheads (usually amounting to approximately 20% of the total costs). In some cases local businesses also make a contribution towards the overhead expenses.

Impact

A number of evaluations of local schemes have been carried out, including several by the consultancy Eysink Smeets and Etman; however, there have been no long-term evaluations. The studies indicate that the schemes do not have a significant impact on levels of crime: in some cases, there appear to have been small reductions in crime, but these examples are countered by instances of increases in crime. However, the findings of surveys of members of the public indicate that the presence of wardens has a positive and sustained impact upon fear of crime. For example, a study by Hauber et al (1993) found that over 75% of a sample of shoppers interviewed said that they were aware of the existence of civic wardens, and over one-third stated that they felt safer as a result of their existence.

The schemes' objective of reducing unemployment has met with some success, in that a proportion of individuals employed as wardens have moved on to permanent employment. In areas with large ethnic minority populations, furthermore, schemes have tended to employ proportionate numbers of ethnic minority staff, which is a crucial factor in developing two-way communication between minorities and the schemes. However, the schemes as a whole are currently facing a recruitment problem, as the better qualified members of the long-term unemployed have, by and large, already been brought into the system.

Aims of warden schemes

The Social Exclusion Unit report introduces the concept of the neighbourhood warden largely in terms of its crime prevention function. However, the broad definition of neighbourhood wardens used in this research, and outlined above, permits the inclusion within the research agenda of schemes which have a wide range of functions and objectives.

The research identified a variety of aims across the 50 schemes reviewed. The majority of these can be reduced to three core issues:

- Crime prevention.
- Environmental improvements.
- Community development.

Within each of the core aims are other elements which shape the characteristics of the schemes (see Figure 1).

Figure 1: Elements of core aims

1. **Crime prevention**
- Reducing levels of crime
- Reducing fear of crime
- Reducing levels of anti-social behaviour

2. **Environmental improvements**
- Improving the general state of repair of properties
- Proactive tackling of vandalism and repairs
- Rapid response to environmental/physical problems
- Improving quality of life for residents

3. **Community development**
- Promoting community solidarity
- Enhancing informal social control
- Increasing levels of employment
- Building confidence in local agencies, including the police
- Promoting intolerance of crime and disorder

The three core aims, and the various elements which comprise them, are inevitably inter-linked. If, following the Social Exclusion Unit report, crime prevention is regarded as the overriding goal of most neighbourhood warden schemes, this in turn demands activities which are environmental and community-oriented. High crime rates in poor neighbourhoods are usually the product of many different and inter-related factors; and 'multiple causes of criminal behavior demand multiple solutions, confronting crime from both foreground (situational) and background (underlying social malaise) perspectives' (Ward, 1997).

Hence, for example, environmental improvements to a housing estate which has previously suffered from a deterioration in the housing stock, poor design, the dumping of litter, and abundant graffiti, might contribute to an emerging sense of attachment to the place on the part of residents, and a corresponding intolerance of local offending.

Likewise, community development initiatives may not have a direct aim of reducing crime, but can have the effect of countering the anti-social behaviour that grows 'where there is apathy and lack of interest in the community, which in itself encourages the small percentage of trouble makers to inflict fear on the majority' (ADC, 1994). For example, community organisations such as residents' associations may become involved in consultations with the police about local initiatives. Crime prevention efforts can be greatly advanced when dialogue starts to develop between the police and communities, in which co-operation with the police has traditionally been condemned as 'grassing' (Morris, 1996). Informal social control can, furthermore, be encouraged by the presence of formal or semi-formal control agencies.

The data on the warden schemes reviewed here clearly demonstrate that such schemes tend to have several, overlapping objectives: most of the schemes have a variety of aims and use a variety of mechanisms to achieve them. The most common theme is one of enhancing the local environment coupled with crime prevention. Almost one half of the schemes (21) cite both environmental improvement and crime prevention as their aims. An example can be found in the Barnsley Community Environment Support Officer employed to encourage improved security in local residential dwellings and commercial premises, promote street clean-up campaigns and ensure that all vacant properties are secure and tidy. Only two of the 50 schemes (namely the Horton Housing Association scheme in Bradford and the HOPE project in Leeds) do not have either an environmental or crime prevention element.

Crime prevention was cited by 31 schemes, or 62%. In most of these cases, the schemes aim to provide an official presence which has a deterrent effect on crime; this is sometimes supplemented by other crime prevention measures. The Chester City Council's Security Service, for example, incorporates a free-phone service ('Vandaline') for tenants to report vandalism or anti-social behaviour, uniformed security patrols, and a concierge service in tower blocks. The uniformed security patrol carried out on the Aylesbury Estate in Southwark (Case Study 2) is one of various initiatives which are aiming to curb the impact of proliferating crime and nuisance in the area.

Almost three-quarters of the schemes – 36 in total – describe one of their objectives as being to improve the environment. This includes tasks such as repairs to local housing stock and care for the external public areas. In the Dacorum Borough Warden Scheme, for example, wardens carry out repairs, litter removal and general maintenance tasks regularly.

Eleven schemes have community development objectives, meaning that they aim to promote mutually supportive and constructive relationships among local residents, and between residents and local agencies. The Manningham Mutual Aid project in Bradford takes the notion of developing a sense of community solidarity to the furthest extent: residents, predominantly of South Asian origin, of this small housing association development were selected with a view to their willingness to provide social support to one another; they signed tenants' contracts confirming this; and they hold regular meetings to air any problems including neighbour disputes.

Another aim closely related to that of community development is to decrease levels of unemployment. Ten schemes have this general aim, which they seek to achieve through hiring local long-term unemployed people as caretakers or wardens or through developing links with the local employment services. The Tenant Support Workers on the Raffles Estate, Carlisle, provide an example of this: they assist tenants to access employment and training opportunities through links with the appropriate agencies.

CASE STUDY 2: Aylesbury Estate Security Patrol, Southwark

Focus and aims

The local authority employs a private security firm to conduct uniformed patrols of the Aylesbury Estate and other council estates in the Taplow neighbourhood. The patrol was introduced in 1994 and covered over 2,200 properties on the Aylesbury estate. It has now been extended to cover the whole of the Taplow neighbourhood, covering 4,515 properties.

The scheme was developed by the local Neighbourhood Manager in consultation with the local tenants' and residents' association. It was proposed in response to fear of crime and high levels of anti-social behaviour, graffiti, general crime, and drug nuisance. The Aylesbury Estate in particular had serious problems of crime, including drug-related crime. The scheme forms part of a wide range of initiatives currently being implemented, and aims to support and complement the Metropolitan Police.

Some physical improvements were also made to the Aylesbury Estate at the time of the introduction of the guards. The demolition of link bridges, according to local police, has had a major impact on crime, as there are now fewer access points to the estate.

Staffing and partnership

The scheme is managed by Taplow Neighbourhood Office. The contract for the security patrols is put out to tender on an annual basis. The service is currently provided by Guarda, which is contracted to supply one supervisor and six patrolling officers who work in shifts patrolling constantly, but numbers increase when the risk is greater. The patrolling officers do not have any special powers. They work in pairs on foot, and carry out letter drops to inform tenants' representatives that they are in the area. They receive some training from the police, which covers 'any person' powers, PACE issues, statement taking, and restraint techniques.

The patrolling officers make reports of incidents, which are kept by the Contracts Manager so that appropriate action can be taken against troublesome residents. A variety of types of incident are dealt with, and include nuisance caused by children and noise problems. Incidents of graffiti and vandalism are reported to the local authority, which is also notified of empty properties.

There is close liaison between the patrol staff and the local home beat police officer. The tenants' and residents' association is also involved in the provision of the service: it assists with evaluation of tenders for the contract, and the patrolling officers' supervisor attends meetings of the association on a regular basis. As part of the scheme a newsletter is distributed, which keeps local people informed of developments.

Costs and funding

The cost of the scheme is £180,000 p.a. Funding is provided by the neighbourhood repairs budget on the grounds that the scheme reduces vandalism and repair costs. The sum available for the scheme has been protected within the budget year on year.

Impact

Crime figures for the area collected by the home beat officer indicate that there has been a reduction in crime in the area. The home beat officer has stated that residents are less likely to be the victim of a burglary or robbery in this area than in any other part of Southwark. Reported crime on the Aylesbury Estate has dropped from approximately 670 incidents in 1997 to 550 incidents in 1998.

The local authority is confident that fear of crime has been considerably reduced, as has been confirmed by tenants in informal discussions. It has been suggested that a major factor in the apparent success of the scheme is the familiarity of the patrolling staff with the area, its people, and the home beat officer.

Methods of achieving aims

As the neighbourhood warden schemes reviewed here have a range of objectives, they employ a range of methods for meeting those objectives. The methods that are most commonly used, and the numbers of schemes which employ them, are presented in Table 1. (It should be noted that many schemes employ more than one method.) A more exhaustive listing of the range of methods that the schemes apply is presented in Figure 2.

Table 1: Methods used to perform functions

Method	Number of schemes
Patrol/Concierge	23
Caretakers	17
Promotion of community organisations	8

As stated above, the three core functions – namely crime prevention, environmental improvements, and community development – of the neighbourhood warden schemes are inter-linked; hence the methods employed are likewise overlapping.

For example, the primary methods used for meeting the crime prevention objective are the employment of patrols and the use of concierges to control access to high-rise blocks.[2]

---

[2]The role of the concierge can vary widely, from being security-oriented to covering social and environmental tasks. However, as the concierge elements of the schemes reviewed here are mostly at the security end of the spectrum – that is, they tend to have the function of guarding entrances to tower-blocks and carrying out surveillance – concierges have been grouped with patrols as one method.

However, many patrols and concierges also fulfil environmental functions to the extent that they seek to take care of void properties, remove litter and graffiti, and carry out minor repairs. The individuals carrying out patrols and acting as concierges can also help to meet community development aims, if they act as a point of contact for residents, and disseminate information about happenings in the locality. The Aylesbury Estate scheme in Southwark (Case Study 2, above) initially began as a security patrol but now includes the distribution of a newsletter and notification of empty properties to the local housing department, as a result of reacting to community need. Some patrols, on the other hand, explicitly have environmental rather than crime prevention objectives: for example, the City Centre Representatives in Glasgow are appointed in order to carry out general cleaning and tidying tasks, notify relevant authorities about environmental problems and provide information on the city to visitors and tourists.

Environmental aims are primarily met by caretakers, but they may also – on either a formal or informal basis – perform other functions, in which case they may be known as 'supercaretakers'. For example, they may play a part in improving security on an estate by providing informal surveillance and liaising with the police; they may provide general support and advice to local residents, thereby enhancing a sense of community; furthermore, they may assist housing managers in preparing void properties for re-letting. For example, the Leeds Federated Housing Association Scheme employs a resident estate worker to oversee the day-to-day maintenance of the housing stock and public areas; in addition, he is frequently the first point of call for tenants who wish to report a crime.

Community development goals, as well as being pursued through the use of patrols, concierges and caretakers as mentioned above, may be furthered by the promotion of community organisations and activities. This may involve the appointment of an officer specifically to play the role of community or neighbourhood development worker. Community organisations such as tenants' and residents' associations are often greatly involved in the initiation and establishment of security patrols or similar schemes, illustrating the close relationship between community development and crime prevention goals.

The aims of crime prevention, environmental improvement and community development can also be furthered by the introduction of active and efficient on-site housing services. Housing management tasks have traditionally included duties such as housing maintenance, provision of information to tenants, re-letting properties, monitoring empty properties, and vetting prospective tenants. It has increasingly been recognised by housing authorities that such tasks can most effectively be achieved through the establishment of housing offices based on or near estates, to which residents and prospective residents have easy access. At the same time, the roles of housing officers are becoming broader, with the effect that they frequently take responsibility for tackling anti-social behaviour, engage in liaison and consultation with residents' associations and other local agencies, and become involved in efforts to address design and environmental problems.

Figure 2: Methods of achieving core aims

1. **Crime prevention**
- Mobile patrols.
- Foot patrols.
- Installation of alarms in empty properties.
- Concierge service – controlling access.
- CCTV.
- Design improvements (e.g. improving lighting; demolishing walk-ways).
- Promotion of Neighbourhood Watch.

2. **Environmental improvements**
- Resident caretaker.
- Localising cleaning services.
- Provision of information to residents regarding repair and maintenance services.
- Liaison with residents to identify environmental/maintenance problems.
- On-going reporting of environmental/maintenance problems to relevant authorities.

3. **Community development**
- Promotion of residents' associations.
- Organisation of events for residents.
- Organisation of activities for young people.
- Provision of a newsletter for residents.
- Consultation with residents over crime prevention/neighbourhood warden initiatives.
- Provision of employment services and training.
- Liaison with health services' information to visitors, and so on.

At least fourteen, or 28%, of the 50 schemes reviewed by this report include some element of localised housing management; in most of these cases, one of the aims is to provide information to residents concerning the various services available to them. On Mitchelhill Estate in Glasgow, on-site management was introduced by Glasgow Housing Department, with the intention of contributing to crime prevention activities, improving standards of care and cleanliness, and ensuring the availability of staff. An example of a scheme where the neighbourhood warden and housing officer roles merge is the Neighbourhood Support Unit (NSU) in Town Hill Estate, Swansea (Case Study 3), which was set up as an extension of the local housing department. NSU workers work from the unit and their housing management functions include monitoring the estate, liaison with the local authority housing department and the installation/removal of radio alarms in void properties.

CASE STUDY 3: Swansea Estate Wardens and Neighbourhood Support Unit

Focus and aims

In 1994 an 'Estate Warden Scheme' covering Townhill North Estate was established, and was extended in 1997 with the establishment of the Neighbourhood Support Unit by the local authority Housing Department. This covers all council housing in Swansea City and Council (approximately 17,000 properties). It employs 20 Neighbourhood Support Workers who provide a 24 hour on-site landlord presence, and have responsibility for maintaining high visibility patrols and installing and monitoring alarms in empty properties.

The driving force behind the original Estate Warden Scheme was the Housing Department's reaction to thefts of heating systems from void properties. Concerns with increasing levels of anti-social behaviour on local authority estates, as well as with void security, led to the establishment of the Neighbourhood Support Unit. A tenant consultation forum was set up to promote tenant involvement, and newsletters continue to keep residents informed of developments.

Staffing and partnership

The role of the Neighbourhood Support Workers includes installing, maintaining and responding to radio alarms; carrying out foot and mobile patrols; witness protection; information gathering; observing anti-social behaviour; reporting crime; communicating with tenants; and court attendance. Training for the staff, provided by the Council and the South Wales Police Authority, covers issues such as offences; civilian powers; communication skills; conflict management and the Crime and Disorder Act.

The Neighbourhood Support Workers do not hold any additional powers to those held by normal citizens. However, as members of the Neighbourhood Support Unit they are able to gather information enabling the local authority to sanction anti-social tenants, for example through evictions.

The scheme has helped to establish stronger working relationships between the Housing Department and many other statutory agencies including the police, Social Services, the Environmental Health Department, the Legal Department, the Youth Justice Team, the Drugs Project and the public at large. The most striking improvement since the inception of the scheme has probably been in terms of the relationship with the police. The collaboration has involved training for local authority staff, the enforcement of housing injunctions and co-operation in problem resolution.

Costs and funding

Neighbourhood Support Workers are employed according to normal employment procedures, and receive annual salaries of £13,000. The cost of the scheme is £600,000 per annum, including staffing, premises and service. A further £460,000 has been spent on the purchase of security screens and radio alarms (complete with the monitoring service).

As the scheme is provided solely for council estates, it is funded solely from the Housing Revenue Account. The local authority is considering extending the scheme to housing associations, to widen the provision of the service and generate an income.

Impact

The Unit appears to have had an impact on anti-social behaviour. To date, 137 anti-social behaviour cases have been referred to the Unit and 34 end of tenancies/evictions have been secured.

A total of 444 alarms are currently in place in vacant properties. The Housing Department is confident that this is a cost-effective means of reducing vandalism and break-ins. From 4.4.98 to 3.2.99 there were 397 attempted break-ins to voids which activated the alarms, saving an estimated £5,000 worth of damage per property.

A more unexpected benefit of the scheme has been the increased capacity to monitor flood levels and to offer support to tenants at times of flooding. The scheme has also provided opportunities for dealing with urgent 'out of hours' housing management issues.

Locations of schemes

Neighbourhood warden schemes can operate in a wide range of different contexts. Those examined by this research cover various housing estates or sections of housing estates, city centres, towns or villages, and entire boroughs.

Two-thirds (33) of warden schemes reviewed here are estate-based. These schemes have been set up in a variety of types of estates; in 18 cases, these are local authority (which can include some housing association and privately owned properties) and, in 15 cases, housing association estates. The available information does not allow an accurate estimate of the sizes of most of these estates. It does, however, indicate that schemes are as likely to exist on very large estates as on small ones. For example, the Aylesbury Estate in Southwark comprises more than 4000 properties, while the Caretaking Plus scheme on Dormanstown West Estate covers approximately 250 properties, and the Manningham Mutual Aid Project only 25 properties.

Four schemes – those in Hyndburn, Glasgow, Hemel Hempstead, and Stockport – cover town or city centre areas which comprise a mixture of residential and public spaces. This type of scheme is typified by the Dutch City Guards, or Stadswacht, model (see Case Study 1), which, while initially intended to target city centres, has increasingly been applied in residential neighbourhoods throughout the Netherlands.

Some schemes cover large areas such as local authority boroughs or groups of towns and villages. For example, the Sedgefield Community Force (Case Study 4) operates at the borough level, covering 54 square miles; the West Mercia Parish Warden Scheme covers 690 parishes; and the St Edmundsbury Borough Council Community Ranger Service covers approximately 34,000 households across the borough.

Finally, while this research has focused on schemes which cover – at least in part – residential areas, warden-type schemes can operate in public areas such as libraries, schools and shopping centres. The Wandsworth Parks Police was set up by the local authority in 1985 for the purpose of enforcing the bye-laws in their parks, and operates from its own control room based in Battersea Park. This scheme is different to the other schemes listed as it is restricted to parks, therefore, residential areas are not included in the scheme and furthermore, they use special powers within the confines of the park. In the Netherlands, uniformed wardens (recruited from the long-term unemployed in a parallel project to the Stadswacht scheme) carry out surveillance on the public transport systems, with the aim of deterring criminal and anti-social behaviour.

CASE STUDY 4: Sedgefield Borough Community Force

Focus and aims

The Sedgefield Community Force is a local authority run force charged with conducting a 24 hour uniformed patrol of the public streets of the local authority area. Sedgefield is a Borough Council with a population of more than 90,000 over 54,000 acres. The introduction of the Force in 1994 was the first stage of a community safety strategy designed by the Council's Community Safety Officer, and was initiated in response to comments from electors during a local election about fear of crime.

The stated objectives of the Force are as follows:
1. To provide a community patrol to increase public safety and reassure the public.
2. To consult with local residents regarding anti-social problems in their area.
3. To consult with local police regarding crime trends and problems, and how the Force can assist in combating them.
4. To provide advice and information to local residents on crime prevention.
5. To obtain and provide evidence of anti-social behaviour in order to assist the relevant enforcement agencies or departments of the Council.
6. To ensure the safety of Council employees whilst undertaking their normal duties.
7. To provide security checks/patrols of Council properties.
8. To generally advise regarding security issues.

Staffing and partnership

The Force consists of 11 patrolling officers and 1 senior patrolling officer, who patrol in marked vehicles and on foot. They operate from a council depot and are in constant radio contact with a control room. They have no special powers, and maintain a nonconfrontational policy of 'observe and report only'. They therefore aim to act as the eyes and ears for the public police, and they immediately inform the police of any incidents.

The officers undergo two weeks of theoretical training and two weeks of practical training. The subjects covered include basic legal knowledge, health and safety, first-aid, situation management and crime prevention. County Durham Constabulary support this training by providing instruction in evidence gathering, scene of crime protection and procedures for bomb threats.

Costs and funding

It is estimated that the overall cost of the scheme is currently £245,050 per annum. It is largely funded by the local authority, with some contribution from the SRB. The overall cost of Sedgefield's Community Safety strategy – which includes Community Force Patrols, Community Neighbourhood Watch, Community Consultation, Community inter-agency initiatives, Community closed circuit television surveillance and Community Rangers – is £400,000 per annum.

Impact

During the first few years of the Force's operation, crime in Sedgefield fell by 20% according to police figures; however, it is assumed that this was at least partially a consequence of the police being more proactive in their attempts to reduce crime. Overall, there is a perception on the part of the Force that its existence assists the police, as it has taken on responsibility for dealing with most minor incidents. Additionally, the Force passes on information to the police which assists them with their intelligence-gathering efforts.

The Force's support staff collect, on a daily basis, data on the Force's activities and contacts. The figures show that over the course of 1998, the Force received 1,877 requests from residents for action on anti-social behaviour, which resulted in 11,136 actions; it dealt with 103 alarm calls; received 67,921 radio calls in its control room (that is, calls from members of the Force and other Council employees); and had 708 contacts of various kinds with the police.

The University of Sheffield has carried out surveys to explore the reactions of the public to the introduction and operation of the Community Force. These show a high level of satisfaction with the service: for example, 6 months after it was set up, one survey found that 83% of respondents felt there was a place for an organisation such as the Force to patrol the streets of Sedgefield. A subsequent customer survey of the quality of service provided by the Force found that 93% of all customers rated the promptness of service as 'excellent' or 'good'; and 95% judged the officers to be 'very helpful' or 'helpful'.

3.   Partnership

Key partners

Since the early 1980s, a broad consensus has emerged that crime prevention can be greatly advanced through effective co-operation and co-ordination between the police, local authorities, and the voluntary and private sectors (LGA, 1997). This approach has been reinforced through the Crime and Disorder Act (1998), which requires that in all areas partnerships are established for the purpose of tackling problems of crime and disorder.

Neighbourhood warden schemes are usually the products of partnerships between various agencies. Most commonly, the agencies involved are local authorities, housing associations, the police, funding bodies, residents' associations, health and employment services, and specialist housing bodies. Partnership working can take place at different levels: for example, in the planning, funding, management, and day-to-day operations of schemes. The links between agencies can be formal, in the sense that the roles and obligations of the partners are specified, or informal, where partners' inputs are spontaneous and variable.

The warden schemes reviewed by this research involve a range of partnerships. Management, however, is primarily carried out by the housing authorities: 21 of the schemes are managed by local authorities, and 17 by housing associations. In two cases, the Priority Estates Project3 provides management support, and in another two cases the schemes are managed by private security companies. West Mercia Parish Warden Scheme is managed by the police. In the remaining cases, management is carried out by partnerships.

There is some police input into most of the schemes that have security functions. The levels of police input vary widely, and in some cases take the form of ongoing but non-formalised support, and in other cases involve formal arrangements. Such relationships usually take the form of close contact with a community liaison officer, such as the Home Beat Officer on the Aylesbury Estate in Southwark (Case Study 2). In many cases, the police make a contribution to the training of security personnel.

Links with other services are difficult to describe, both because they can manifest in many different ways and because of a lack of information. However, several schemes have links with the National Health Service and/or with local employment services. The NHS links tend to take the form of contact with a local day centre or services for the elderly. The Horton Housing Association Community Support Agency, for example, has a Care Programme for clients with severe and enduring mental health problems, who are a priority for Social Services and the Health Authority. The scheme has been very successful at reducing hospital re-admissions, preventing mental health crises and assisting people to establish footholds in their communities.

---

[3] The Priority Estates Project acts in conjunction with local authorities and tenants in seeking to improve the delivery of housing services, with a particular focus on the establishment of on-site housing management.

Links with employment services tend to exist where schemes have the specific objective of decreasing local unemployment through hiring and training local people to work on the schemes or providing local residents with access to training or employment opportunities. The Ashiana Housing Association Residential Support Worker encourages residents to gain work experience by contributing to the project.

Local residents, usually acting through residents' associations, can be the most important partners involved in warden schemes. As those who experience first-hand the problems of a local area, whether these be related to crime, environmental decline, or other factors, residents often have most to contribute to the initiation, design and implementation of projects. The activities of the residents' association of Hartlepool's Central Estate (Case Study 5) – which has set up a Neighbourhood Watch scheme, and has a close relationship with the local home beat officer – appear to have had success in bringing down a previously high crime rate on the estate, which had caused much anxiety and a sense of powerlessness among residents.

CASE STUDY 5: Central Estate, Hartlepool

Focus and aims

Central Estate is a mainly local authority run estate, which comprises approximately 600 properties, and includes family houses, sheltered bungalows for older residents, and flats for single people – a mix of housing type which, coupled with a lack of facilities for young children and teenagers, has produced conflicting needs and internal tensions. From the late 1980s to the mid 1990s the estate suffered high levels of crime and unemployment, and was described as a problem area by the local press. Voids on the estate reached a maximum of 101.

In 1994 the estate's residents' association conducted a survey to assess local problems. Ninety-two per cent of the 420 respondents stated that they lived in fear of crime, and 75% that they had been a victim of crime on the estate in the past two years. A large majority of respondents stated that they supported the introduction of security patrols, but this did not materialise because of a lack of funds.

A number of initiatives have sought to address the problems of Central Estate, which were mainly prompted by the active residents' association founded in 1991. In 1996 a 'dedicated' police officer was placed on the estate in response to pressure from the residents' association. The initiatives also include the establishment of an on-site housing office (employing an estate caretaker among others), the appointment of a Community Development Worker by the residents' association, the introduction of 'Neighbourhood Watch', and the installation of a CCTV camera over the shop located in the middle of the estate. SRB funding has been acquired for design improvements, including landscaping, and work to 'design out crime'.

Staffing and partnership

The initiatives on Central Estate are coordinated by the Community Development Worker and are community-led. Three key partners are involved:
- Central Residents' Association
- Hartlepool Police – West View Community Team and Neighbourhood Watch
- 9.5

The level of trust between the three agencies is such that not only do they meet regularly but are able to ring each other informally whenever the need arises.

Costs and funding

There are various sources of funding including SRB, the local authority and the National Lottery Charities Board. Information about the overall cost of the various initiatives is unavailable. The cost of employing the Community Development Worker is £55,000 over a three-year period.

Impact

There has been a marked decrease in crime on Central Estate. Police figures show a drop of 35.5% in recorded crime from 1994 to 1997. There were 36 recorded crimes in February 1994 compared to 4 in February 1998. Residential burglaries reduced by 88% from 1994 to 1997. There has also been an increase in the number of lettings and a decrease in the numbers of voids and terminations.

The perception of the residents' association is that the major factors in the local initiative's success have been their combination of tough policing, good liaison between the residents' association and the police, improved housing management, and the involvement of the Community Development Worker.

Employment status of wardens

The majority of the schemes reviewed for this study did not provide information about the employment status of wardens. However, from the information that is available, it appears that most wardens employed by the schemes tend to be low paid and are appointed according to standard employment procedures. At least eight of the schemes have a specific aim of recruiting from the local long-term unemployed and providing the staff with training that will assist them in taking up permanent positions in the future. The Eldonians scheme, which has recently been established in Liverpool, intends to recruit from the long-term unemployed: that is, individuals who have been unemployed for at least 12 months. The Gipsyville Estate Warden project in Hull has links with the Government's New Deal initiative.

In some cases, including the Headrow Housing Group 'liaison tenant' scheme in Leeds (Case

Study 6), wardens do not hold salaried positions, but receive a small reduction in rent in return for the services they provide – usually in the form of social support – to fellow-residents. Where wardens (whether salaried or not) play some kind of supportive role, it can be most appropriate for them to live 'on-site'. Where schemes are serviced by people resident in the area, this can encourage a sense of ownership of, and hence commitment to the schemes among local people. For example, the resident caretaker employed by the Leeds Federated Housing Association is able to assist tenants in dealing with emergencies of all kinds in addition to carrying out routine maintenance tasks, because he can be easily contacted. In cases where wardens primarily have a crime prevention role difficulties may arise if they are local residents, since they or their families may face intimidation. However, there need not be a conflict per se between local residents and wardens involved in this type of role; the effect may be positive and their presence may help to discourage intimidation.

CASE STUDY 6: Headrow Housing Group Liaison Tenant Scheme, Yorkshire

Focus and aims

The Headrow Housing Group runs Liaison Tenant Schemes at nine developments in Yorkshire. These schemes aim to provide, at low cost, an on-site presence in order to allay fear of crime and offer support to vulnerable tenants. They involve the appointment of liaison tenants, who receive a small reduction in their rents in return for providing a 'good neighbour' service.

The housing developments vary in size, with the largest comprising 69 properties. Across the schemes, 75% of tenants are elderly. The scheme arose out of discussions between housing staff and tenants about how support could best be offered to tenants, especially those who are vulnerable.

Staffing and partnership

The role of the liaison tenants varies in accordance with the needs of the developments in which they are based. In general, they act as a communication link between the housing association and its tenants, deal with out-of-hours emergencies – for example, responding to repair requests and calling the emergency services – and visit vulnerable tenants. They receive training covering issues such as their role and responsibilities, health and safety, and housing policies and procedures.

Recruitment is undertaken jointly by the Group and tenants. Given the nominal rewards, it is difficult to attract new liaison tenants and retain existing ones. Tenants play an active role in drawing up the list of duties of the liaison tenant, and in the selection procedures.

Partnership is seen as essential to a successful scheme. The partners involved, and their levels of involvement, vary from development to development. Partners include the housing and social services, voluntary services, the police, and the Church.

Costs and funding

The cost has been estimated at £1,000 p.a. per liaison tenant, excluding inputs of partners. The cost arises from the rent reduction, business calls, and transport and training expenses. It is paid for by a service charge which must be agreed with tenants. The service charge varies between the developments, and is, for example, £0.55 per unit per week on Ashdown Close, which comprises 18 properties.

Impact

Although no formal evaluation has taken place, Headrow Housing claims that in most cases the scheme has proved sustainable, helps to reduce tenancy turnover, improves the quality of life of tenants (especially those who are vulnerable), and reduces numbers of incidents of crime and other anti-social behaviour.

Funding

Approximately one quarter (12) of the schemes are funded by more than one source. The main funding organisation is the local authority which funds almost half of the schemes (23) at least partially. For 18 of the schemes in receipt of local authority funding, this is their sole source of funding. Sixteen schemes are funded at least partially by a housing association, seven by tenant charges, and five by the Single Regeneration Budget. The remaining schemes are funded by various sources, such as Innovation and Good Practice (Housing Corporation) Grants, charitable funds or the European Union.

While little information is available on the costs of most of the schemes, it is clear that they range from those which are funded to a high level to those which depend on substantial voluntary efforts on the part of local people. Among the schemes included in this report as case studies, for example, Swansea's Estate Warden and Neighbourhood Support Unit scheme has an annual cost of £600,000; and Headrow Housing Group's Liaison Tenant scheme costs approximately £1,000 per liaison tenant per annum.

As Table 2 demonstrates, local authorities are most likely to fund projects aimed at reducing crime and disorder (70%, or 16, of the schemes with local authority funding have some crime prevention function). Newport's Estate Ranger Service (Case Study 7), for example, is funded by the local authority's Housing Revenue Account, and was set up with the specific aim of reducing anti-social behaviour. Approximately half of the housing association-funded schemes (12 in total) incorporate environmental objectives. Only 5 schemes with community development objectives are funded by this source.

Housing association funds are most likely to be used for schemes with environmental improvement components: 14 schemes, or 88% of those with housing association funding, include this function. Table 2 shows also that of the 7 schemes funded (at least partially) by tenant charges, 5 have environmental improvement functions (for example, Brunel Housing's Caretakers Scheme is funded by a service charge of £2.46 per week per tenant), and 2 crime prevention functions. The 5 schemes funded by the Single Regeneration Budget cover all three core functions.

Table 2: Funding source by objective of neighbourhood warden scheme

FUNDING SOURCE No. of Schemes	FUNCTIONS[4]		
	CRIME PREVENTION (%)	ENVIRONMENTAL IMPROVEMENTS (%)	COMMUNITY DEVELOPMENT (%)
LOCAL AUTHORITY 23	16 (70)	12 (52)	5 (22)
HOUSING ASSOCIATION 16	5 (31)	14 (88)	5 (31)
TENANT CHARGE 7	2 (29)	5 (71)	0 (0)
SINGLE REGENERATION BUDGET 5	4 (80)	3 (60)	2 (40)

Table 3 presents the funding source by methods used. It shows that 15 of the 23 local

Table 3: Funding source by method of neighbourhood warden scheme

FUNDING SOURCE No. of Schemes	METHODS[5]		
	PATROL/ CONCIERGE (%)	CARETAKER (%)	PROMOTION OF COMMUNITY ORGANISATIONS (%)
LOCAL AUTHORITY 23	15 (65)	4 (17)	4 (17)
HOUSING ASSOCIATION 16	1 (6)	11 (69)	2 (13)
TENANT CHARGE 7	2 (40)	4 (57)	0 (0)
SINGLE REGENERATION BUDGET 5	4 (80)	3 (60)	2 (40)

[4]Schemes with more than one function are counted more than once.
[5]Schemes with more than one method are counted more than once; those few schemes that do not use any of the three major methods are not counted in these columns.

authority-funded schemes employ patrols or concierges, as does just 1 of the 16 housing association-funded schemes. Eleven, or over two-thirds, of the local authority-funded schemes employ a caretaker.

CASE STUDY 7: Newport Estate Ranger Service

Focus and aims

The Newport Estate Ranger Service was established in 1994 by the Borough Council, in response to the growing problems of anti-social behaviour on estates and the increasing number of complaints from tenants. It is dedicated to preventing anti-social behaviour – such as excessive noise, threatening behaviour, joy-riding, vandalism and neighbour disputes. Incidents of crime are immediately reported to the police; therefore the activities of the rangers filter out those incidents where a police presence is not required or is not an appropriate use of resources.

The service was originally restricted to Council estates (approximately 12,500 properties), and has been expanded to included Charter Housing Association estates (a further 1,600 properties). The service therefore caters for about 25% of the Borough population.

Staffing and partnership

A team of 12 Rangers operates 2 shifts per day, 7 days a week, from 8 am to midnight. The rangers wear a low-key uniform, and patrol in Council vehicles. They can be diverted to incidents by radio messages sent from a centralised control centre which accepts calls from the public. Staff receive a two week induction course, and on-going training under qualified supervision.

The Rangers aim to prevent anti-social behaviour through their presence, and to stop the escalation of incidents through informal persuasion. Furthermore, evidence is gathered on anti-social tenants for the Housing Officer who can take legal action if required. The Rangers have no special powers, and aim to nip problems of anti-social behaviour in the bud without showing an excessive reaction in order to improve the atmosphere on the estates.

The relationship of the scheme with the police is very effective; informal liaison takes place at all levels but most commonly in the form of Ranger/Constable interaction. A formal protocol has recently been drawn up with the police which allows for the passing of information on specific cases. There is also informal liaison with community groups including Neighbourhood Watch groups.

Costs and funding

The service is funded through the local authority's Housing Revenue Account. Costs are currently approximately £300,000 per annum, which is equivalent to 49p per week per tenant. The scheme was initially set up with a Housing Initiatives grant.

Impact

97% of the 8,600 calls taken from January 1998 to March 1999 were dealt with within an hour; and calls cost an average of £36.58 to deal with. The figure of 8,600 cases shows an increase of 29% on the previous year. The incidents are broken down into three main categories: anti-social behaviour (83%), management tasks (11%), and security (6%). About 150 of the incidents were reported to the police.

A sample of 1,000 residents were surveyed about their response to the Ranger Service, of whom 66% regarded it as a good thing.

Is there a typical neighbourhood warden scheme?

This review has described 50 schemes with a host of different objectives, methods of meeting those objectives, funders and managers. It is clear is that there is no single model of neighbourhood warden scheme in operation. There are, however, common threads running through the existing schemes (see Figure 3).

Environmental improvements and crime prevention tend to be the main objectives of neighbourhood warden schemes. The schemes tend to be based on either local authority or housing association housing estates but can exist in town centres or indeed cover large geographical areas. As such, a scheme is as likely to exist in one residential block in a town as to cover a whole town.

Local authorities are the main funders of schemes, but there is evidence to suggest that many are funded by a variety of sources, pointing towards the development of partnerships. Local authorities appear to fund mainly crime prevention or environmental improvement schemes and, as a result, patrol and caretaker schemes.

Figure 3: *Methods of neighbourhood warden schemes*

Functions
●   Mainly crime prevention and environmental improvements.
●   A proportion incorporate community development aims.

Methods
●   Security patrols/concierges.
●   Caretaker/supercaretaker.
●   Promotion of community organisations.

Funding
●   Mainly local authority and housing association.
●   Many schemes involve a partnership approach to both funding and management.

Locations
●   Mainly based on local authority and housing association estates.
●   Some schemes cover boroughs, parishes, towns, cities.

The schemes' objectives dictate the methods employed by the key partners in seeking to achieve them.

4.   Evaluation

Findings of existing evaluations

The large majority of schemes reviewed for this report have not undertaken any evaluations of their performance. In at least 16 cases, however, there has been some monitoring of their impact or effectiveness. This takes various forms; examining police data for evidence of the schemes' impact on crime, conducting surveys of residents' opinions on the schemes and fear of crime, assessing cost-effectiveness, and considering data from Housing Departments on numbers of void properties and lettings.

Some of these evaluations indicate that the schemes have had success in reducing levels of recorded crime. Police data suggest that, among the case studies, the Aylesbury Estate, Sedgefield, and Hartlepool Central Estate schemes have had a positive impact on crime rates.6 Of the other schemes considered by this research, those on the Alma Road, Broadwater Farm and Kingsmead estates (all in London), and on the Mitchelhill and Possil Park estates (both in Glasgow) also appear to have had some success in this respect. However, in most of these cases crime figures in themselves tell us little about the effectiveness of wardens or patrols per se, as these tend to be elements of wider crime prevention strategies, which include enhanced enforcement.

Those schemes which have sought to monitor their performance by conducting opinion surveys within the local populations can claim to have enjoyed some success. The Sedgefield Community Force and Newport's Estate Ranger Service appear to be largely popular among local people; and the Dutch Stadswacht schemes have been effective in reducing fear of crime. The impact of Glasgow City Centre Representatives was assessed by means of surveys of city centre users and businesses, which showed that 80% of the public felt the project was a good idea, and 70% that the CCRs 'help make Glasgow a friendlier place'. A 1995 survey on the Wandsworth Parks Police found that 90% of respondents regarded the scheme as a very good idea, and over 75% thought that the police were courteous, helpful and efficient. Likewise, surveys in the areas piloting the West Mercia Parish Warden Scheme indicated that it was largely valued by local people.

Few conclusions can be reached about the cost-effectiveness of existing schemes, since evaluations tend not to measure any savings accrued to housing authorities or the police against the overall costs of the schemes. Swansea's Neighbourhood Support Unit is confident that savings have been made through the use of radio alarms to prevent break-ins to empty properties. A Priority Estates Project evaluation of the Caretaking Plus schemes piloted in Kemsley Village and Dormanstown West suggested that the schemes produced net savings on repairs and other costs.7

6Further details on the effectiveness of the case study schemes are included in the individual discussions of these schemes, above.

The Possil Park Community Business scheme in Glasgow was monitored by two City Council exercises over 7 years. It was found that between 1989 and 1990 the project made an estimated net saving of £57,995 in reduced costs arising from vandalism to and theft from empty dwellings (Osborn and Shaftoe, 1995).

Housing data on numbers of voids, average lengths of tenancies, rates of tenancy terminations and so on can be a clear indication of whether an estate is broadly perceived as being in decline or, conversely, has acquired a good reputation. On Hartlepool's Central Estate, the drop in levels of recorded crime appears to have helped to make the estate more popular, as there has been an increase in the number of lettings and a decrease in the numbers of voids and terminations. On Hackney's Kingsmead estate, lower levels of crime were accompanied by a 76% reduction in the number of voids from April 1993 to May 1995 (Morris, 1996). Similarly, voids on Glasgow's Mitchelhill estate fell between 1988 and 1991, during which period crime had fallen, and a waiting-list was established of people who had specifically requested a move on to the estate (SNU, 1994).

For the most part, the attempts to monitor the performance of the existing warden schemes are extremely limited in terms of both their scope and their quality. It is therefore not possible to make any broad judgements on the basis of these evaluations about which elements of schemes work and which do not, or whether broad or narrowly focused schemes are more successful. However, some general conclusions about effectiveness have been advanced by published material examining the impact of housing-based initiatives – including some appearing in this review of projects – aimed at arresting social and economic decline and reducing crime.

There is evidence that the introduction of decentralised housing management, involving, for example, an estate-based housing office responsible for organising repairs, lettings, and rent collection locally, can be beneficial. Foster and Hope (1993) evaluated the introduction of the Priority Estates Project (PEP) localised housing management model to two local authority estates in Hull and London, which appeared to lead to some reductions in crime and disorder. Power and Tunstall's review of change on 20 deprived housing estates (1995) also concludes that localised services have the effect of raising 'the general standards of an estate, making the estate as an area more acceptable'.

The localisation of housing management services is often carried out alongside efforts to increase residents' involvement in organising and developing services. Extended resident participation of this kind is highlighted by Power and Turnstall as a critical factor in successful initiatives. A focus on management change and a commitment to participation are also elements of a number of successful crime prevention initiatives on housing estates highlighted by a 1993 Safe Neighbourhoods Unit (SNU) report.

---

[7]For example, the cost of 12 repairs by the Village Officer appointed by Caretaking Plus in Kemsley Village was £202.38, whereas 12 repairs by an external contractor would have been £453.17, suggesting an annual net saving to the housing association of over £4,000. In Dormanstown West, the scheme reduced the void turnaround time from 6 to 3.9 weeks, producing a total annual saving to the local authority of £51,660 on lost rent, repair costs and security guard costs.

Foster and Hope's evaluation of PEP points to the fact that local initiatives will be successful in fostering community support and achieving their wider goals only if there is high quality implementation. In the case of the London project that they studied, participation of local residents was hindered by the fact that the initial housing team leader was perceived as unsympathetic. Further demoralisation of local people occurred when the PEP consultancy temporarily withdrew from the estate, partially because of poor quality management.

It is clear that the introduction of localised management, extended resident participation, and effective implementation will not necessarily, in themselves, produce a reduction in crime and improved social and economic conditions on a deprived estate. Other types of social change in the local area inevitably have an impact upon patterns of crime and deprivation. One part of the Hull estate examined by Foster and Hope experienced an increase in crime, which appeared to be related to an influx of new, young tenants. On the London estate, tensions among residents remained high, and crime rates continued to be quite volatile although they dropped overall. Here, the turnover of residents and the social heterogeneity of the population seemed to inhibit the exercise of informal control over disorderly behaviour.

Farr and Osborn's (1997) report on various concierge schemes in high-rise blocks illustrates the inter-play between different aspects of housing policy and patterns. This report indicates that the presence of concierges can be effective in reducing crime and improving conditions within blocks; however, improvements are also dependent upon other factors. Because they are in a position to control access, concierges are clearly able to have a greater impact upon problems emanating from outside their blocks than on problems within them, and hence, for example, changes in allocations policies will have an independent effect. Thus Farr and Osborn suggest that concierge schemes may be most valuable in helping to create conditions in which maximum advantage can be gained from other changes.

In general, the published literature points to the importance of combining measures to combat crime and deprivation: management, design, security, economic and community development components can complement and enhance each other. The implementation of a variety of measures of course necessitates effective inter-agency working. It is also crucial that the various elements of a strategy are sustained: if, for example, funding problems lead to the abandonment of a key element of a scheme, problems which might have seemed under control can quickly resurface (Osborn and Shaftoe, 1995). On the other hand, some measures may specifically be designed as short-term, intensive inputs, the effects of which can be bolstered and extended through the introduction of other, longer-term strategies.

All initiatives, of course, operate within a wider social and economic context. Unemployment, discrimination, changes in family structures, and other broad processes can lead to the marginalisation of the most deprived groups in society. Power and Turnstall found increasing polarisation on the poorest council estates, resulting in particular from the fact that 'many households ... had lost all connection with the job market' (1995). They found also that racial discrimination had helped to create concentrations of disadvantage. While local strategies can have the effect of mitigating polarisation, their potential benefits are necessarily constrained by underlying economic and social problems. Thus the importance of linking local strategies to broader-based policies, for example on employment, cannot be over-emphasised.

The need for evaluation

It is crucial that neighbourhood warden schemes are evaluated. Clearly, thorough evaluations permit those who are planning and implementing schemes to learn from the successes and failures of others. However, the wide range of projects reviewed by this research demonstrates that it is not possible to propose a single model of evaluation. Just as the schemes themselves should be tailored to the specific needs and problems of the area to which they are to be introduced, so also should the design of evaluations be carefully matched to the scheme's specific objectives and methods. Furthermore, the evaluation must take into account the need to gather detailed information about all aspects of the scheme.

Many of the schemes reviewed by this project are multi-dimensional, in that they seek to perform more than one objective and/or employ more than one method. Evaluations should therefore not proceed on the basis of a single measure of success. Furthermore, measures of success should themselves be multi-faceted: for example, where an initiative has the primary goal of crime prevention, it would probably be inappropriate for an evaluation to examine only changes in the overall rate of crime in the local area. The initiative may lead to a reduction in one form of crime but not others; or it may reduce levels of fear of crime but not levels of actual crime (as has been the result of many of the Dutch Stadswacht schemes).

Table 4, summarises the wide number of ways in which the achievement of a scheme's objectives can be measured; it is adapted from a list proposed by an SNU report (1994) on the development of concierge schemes and controlled access in high-rise blocks.

In cases where measures such as those highlighted by Table 4 indicate that a scheme has met certain objectives, it is also crucial that the evaluation can link the noted improvements to specific aspects of the scheme. For example, access to continuous monitoring data should enable evaluators to determine exactly when a fall in crime has occurred, and hence to identify the key factors leading to this decline (SNU, 1993).

Of those evaluations of warden schemes that have been carried out to date, most have been retrospective. Process evaluations – which should be built into schemes from the very outset, and involve the collection of good quality base-line data – allow key partners to identify problems and benefits of schemes as they arise, and to modify elements accordingly. Furthermore, where it can be demonstrated that a given scheme is successful, all those involved (including local residents) may be encouraged to offer further support and contribution.

A difficulty faced by evaluators is that certain potential benefits of many schemes are intangible: for example, there can be no definitive measure of the extent to which a project promotes feelings of community solidarity among local residents. In such cases, evaluators

Table 4: Methods of evaluation

Objective	Measure
Crime and security	Levels of particular crimes/incidents. Overall crime/incident rate. Levels of fear of crime. Levels of anti-social behaviour (such as noise, littering, graffiti).
Lettability	Requests for transfers on to or off an estate/housing development. Void levels. Average duration of vacancies.
Repair and management performance	Percentage of rent collected. Time taken over repairs and maintenance tasks. Residents' satisfaction with performance. Assessment of external appearance of properties and common areas.
Resident satisfaction	'Before and after' residents' survey measuring. • Does the scheme live up to expectations? • Are residents more or less prepared to remain on the estate/housing development? • Residents' views on the scheme. • Residents' views on housing and allied services.
Staff satisfaction	Staff interviews should investigate: • Does the scheme live up to expectations? • Staff views on different elements of the scheme. • Staff views on performance of their own and other services.
Resident participation	Extent of resident involvement in management. Extent of resident involvement in community affairs. Number and activities of community organisations.

should consider the use of qualitative methodologies, such as in-depth interviews with key participants, which can provide useful insights into ongoing developments.

Notwithstanding the intangibility of many objectives of schemes, it may be extremely important for evaluations to incorporate some form of cost-benefit analysis, in order that funders can establish whether their schemes provide value for money and should be offered further funding. 'Value for money' can itself, of course, take many different forms: for example, substantial savings can be made from reducing break-ins, and hence damage, to void properties (as achieved by Swansea's Neighbourhood Support Unit); or from using an extended caretaking service to undertake repairs rather than an external contractor (see, for example, the case of 'Caretaking Plus' in Dormanstown West and Kemsley Village).

However, in assessing the 'value for money' of a scheme, any general changes in housing policy must be taken account of; for example, repairs and maintenance costs on an estate may rise if the buildings had been neglected in the period leading up to the scheme's implementation (SNU, 1994). Another complicating factor is the time-scale of the project and its projected impact: it is inevitably a complex matter to assess the longer-term monetary benefits of a scheme which ultimately aims to reduce unemployment in a deprived area by making the area more attractive to businesses.

In most cases, indeed, the question of time-scale is crucial. A thorough evaluation is likely to be conducted over the longer rather than the shorter term, since the impact of a given scheme will probably vary over time, as will the problems that it seeks to address. Likewise, certain elements of a scheme – for example, community development elements – may evolve over many years, while others may produce intense but short-lived activity. This demands that evaluators – as Crawford (1998) suggests with respect to crime prevention evaluations in general – should not assume that there is a distinct end point to their research, but should be prepared 'to go beyond the pre-test/post-test model and involve residents in monitoring and evaluating effects on an ongoing basis.'

The importance of including resident feedback as an element of evaluations cannot be over-stated, since the success of any scheme is ultimately dependent upon, and has its major impact on, local people. However, it must be recognised that resident response to surveys is frequently low; therefore incentives for respondents may have to be considered. In areas where the population is highly mixed, for example in terms of age or ethnicity, it is important that opinion surveys produce information about a cross-section of residents, as schemes may have differential impacts on the various groupings.

Evaluations of partnership initiatives must recognise that partnership is not an end in itself: as Bright (1997) has argued with respect to local crime prevention strategies, 'Partnerships, steering groups and multi-agency committees do not prevent crime. They talk about preventing crime'. Hence evaluations of multi-agency schemes must seek to identify concrete achievements (or hindrances met) by the partnerships, and the conditions under which partnership working is most effective. Effectiveness may be enhanced if there is an onus on all partners to assist evaluators by providing information relating to their own areas of responsibility. For example, the police can provide data on reported crime, and housing departments can make available data on void properties and lettings.

Displacement is a potential problem faced by most locally-based crime prevention strategies. Evaluations of neighbourhood warden schemes with crime prevention aims should therefore seek – insofar as it is possible – to assess the extent to which the schemes have the effect of displacing, rather than eliminating, criminal and anti-social behaviour. For example, it should be taken into account that where local authorities and the police act in partnership to evict 'problem families' from council estates, there is a danger that these families will cause difficulties in whatever area they then move to. (Dundee City Council's Families Project has specifically sought to address this problem, by working with, rather than simply moving on, 'problem families'.)

5.   Conclusions

It is clear from the research findings reported upon here that existing neighbourhood warden schemes in Britain vary enormously in terms of the problems they address, the methods they employ, their scale and funding, and the agencies involved in them. This diversity, and the lack of thorough evaluations of existing schemes, makes it difficult to draw out firm conclusions about the strengths and weaknesses of current initiatives, or to propose specific guidelines that should be followed by those seeking to establish new schemes.

The Home Office Policing and Reducing Crime Unit is commissioning research to fill this gap by conducting thorough evaluations of a small sample of neighbourhood warden schemes. The research will analyse the impact of the schemes on levels of crime and disorder and the quality of life in local areas, assess the cost-effectiveness of schemes, and identify elements of good practice in the planning and implementation of schemes.

However, the evidence cited in this report – based on the findings of research visits, and the limited monitoring and evaluation exercises that have been carried out to date – does suggest that warden schemes can help to address many of the problems faced by deprived neighbourhoods. It appears that schemes, often in conjunction with other local crime prevention initiatives, can contribute to bringing down levels of crime and fear of crime. Warden schemes which encompass environmental and community-based aims, perhaps together with crime prevention elements, can help to reverse the social and physical decline of poor areas. In drawing on the skills, expertise and good-will of a variety of local individuals and agencies, many schemes engage in constructive and wide-ranging partnership activities which have tangible impacts upon lives.

On the basis of the findings of this review, and what is already known about successful crime prevention and related activities, it is possible to propose some general recommendations that should be followed in developing and implementing a scheme. In sum, the recommendations presented below emphasise the importance of developing schemes which are suited to the characteristics of the areas in which they are based, and hence the need for information, communication, and community involvement at every stage of the process.

● Establish the precise geographic parameters of the scheme, and the problems within those parameters which the scheme is intended to address. Use the findings of the local crime and disorder audit, and any other more localised surveys of environmental and social problems, in order to identify the specific nature and scope of local problems.

- Once the specific aims and parameters of the scheme have been established, consider the full range of means – within the limits set by resources, and the competencies of the key agencies involved – by which these might be achieved. Take into account the fact that local problems, and hence some of the potential solutions, are likely to be inter-connected and overlapping.

- Involve local people in all aspects of the scheme's design and implementation including problem identification, through public consultations and liaison with Neighbourhood Watch, residents' associations, and other community groups. Involvement of local people may be advanced through the consultations carried out by local community safety partnerships engaged in producing crime and disorder audits and strategies. Local people may have clear ideas about what the scheme needs to achieve and how it may be able to do so; and they may be able to play an active part in it as members of staff. Ensure representation of as wide a spectrum of the local population as possible – in terms of age, ethnicity and gender – in consultations and the staffing of the scheme.

- Recognise that partnership is likely to be a crucial component of the scheme. Establish the specific inputs that can be made by all available partners, and clarify the roles and obligations of each from the outset. Police input on a formal or informal level can be extremely valuable, for example, in the training of wardens or where wardens and local home beat officers liase regularly. An ACPO convened group, 'Working the Beat', has recently drawn up a set of 'Fundamental Principles' which set out the basis on which it considers the police can engage with the development of warden type schemes (See Appendix B).

- Ensure that there is good communication between all partners so that problems and concerns can be addressed at an early stage.

- Monitor the implementation of the scheme, in order that problems can be identified, and wherever possible addressed, as and when they arise. Ensure from the outset that the impact and cost-effectiveness of the scheme can be properly assessed: for example, by collecting base-line data, and costing the inputs of all key agencies.

References

Association of District Councils (1994) *Winning Communities: The Role of Housing in Promoting Community Safety.* London: ADC.

Bright, J. (1997) *Turning the Tide: Crime, Community and Prevention.* London: Demos.

Crawford, A. (1998) *Crime Prevention and Community Safety.* Harlow: Longman.

Farr, J. and Osborn, S. (1997) *High Hopes: Concierge, Controlled Entry and Similar Schemes for High Rise Blocks.* DoE Housing Research Report. London: The Stationery Office.

Foster, J. and Hope. T. (1993) *Housing, Community and Crime: The Impact of the Priority Estates Project.* Home Office Research Study 131. London: HMSO.

Hauber, A., Hofstra, B., Toornvliet, L. and Zandbergen, A. (1996) 'Some New Forms of Functional Social Control in the Netherlands and their Effects', *British Journal of Criminology*, 36 (2) 199–219.

Laycock, G. and Tilley, N. (1995) *Policing and Neighbourhood Watch: Strategic Issues.* Crime Detection and Prevention Series, Paper 60. London: Home Office Police Research Group.

Local Government Association and Local Government Management Board (1997) *Crime – The Local Solution: Current Practice.* London: LGBM.

Morris, S. (1996) *Policing Problem Housing Estates.* Crime Detection and Prevention Series Paper 74. London: Home Office Police Research Group.

Osborn, S. and Shaftoe, H. (1995) *Safer Neighbourhoods? Successes and Failures in Crime Prevention.* London: Safe Neighbourhoods Unit.

Power, A. and Tunstall, R. (1995) *Swimming Against the Tide: Polarisation or Progress on 20 Unpopular Council Estates, 1980-1995.* York: Joseph Rowntree Foundation.

Safe Neighbourhoods Unit (1993) *Crime Prevention on Council Estates.* London: HMSO.

Safe Neighbourhoods Unit (1994) *High Expectations: A Guide to the Development of Concierge Schemes and Controlled Access in High Rise Social Housing.* London: HMSO.

Ward, C.M. (1997) 'Community Crime Prevention: Addressing the Background and Foreground Causes of Criminal Behavior', *Journal of Criminal Justice,* 25 (1): 1-18.

APPENDIX A: OVERVIEW OF THE SCHEMES

Scheme	Functions	Methods	Duration	Area covered	No. of staff	Funding	Management	Evaluation/ monitoring
1. Alma Road Estate, Enfield	Crime prevention; environmental improvement; security patrol.	Concierge; liaison with police, tenants; on-site management	1986-	Local authority estate	No information	Local authority	Local authority	Yes
2. Ashiana Housing Association Resident Support Worker, Rochdale	Crime prevention; environmental improvement; community development	Caretaker; employment services; on-site management	Recent	Housing association properties throughout Rochdale	1	Ashiana Housing Association	Housing association	No
3. Aylesbury Estate Security Patrols, Southwark	Crime prevention	Security patrol (close liaison with local Home Beat Officer, Housing Office and Tenants' Association)	1994-	7 local authority estates – 4,500 housing units with 12,000 residents	7	Local authority	GUARDA – private security company	No
4. Barnsley Community Environment Support Officer	Crime prevention; environmental improvement; community development	Combines aspects of caretaker and community development worker; on-site management	1995-	Village of Grimesthorpe	1	SRB Metropolitan Housing Association; Chantry Housing Association	Housing association	No
5. Bentilee Community Housing Estate Caretaker Service, Stoke-on-Trent	Crime prevention; environmental improvement	Estate caretaker	Dec 1998-	Housing association estates	No information	Britiania charitable foundation Bentilee	Community Housing Ltd	Pending
6. Broadwater Farm Estate 'Supercaretaker' scheme, Haringey	Environmental improvement	Caretaker; liaison with tenants and local services; on-site management	1983-	Local authority estate – 1,063 dwellings	8	Local authority	No information	Yes
7. Brunel Housing – Caretakers Scheme, Bradford	Crime prevention; environmental improvement	Caretaker; liaison with housing management	Late 1980s-	Housing association – collection of 295 Victorian terraced dwellings	No information	Service charge	Housing association	Pending

APPENDIX A: OVERVIEW OF THE SCHEMES (continued)

Scheme	Functions	Methods	Duration	Area covered	No. of staff	Funding	Management	Evaluation/ monitoring
8. Camden Caretaking Service	Environmental improvement	Extended caretaking service; duties include visiting vulnerable tenants; liaison with estate officers and the police	1994-	Local authority estates across Borough	?	Local authority	Local authority	No
9. Clayton Brooks Estate Team, Lancashire	Environmental improvement	'Supercaretaker' type scheme with local residents, mainly long term unemployed who repair, clean and decorate. They also provide 'eyes and ears' for the local authority.	1998	Housing association estate includes 1000 properties	10	Housing association maintenance budget and tenant service charge.	Housing association	The process of employing from unemployed residents has been evaluated.
10. Chester City Council Security Services	Crime prevention	Security patrol; concierge scheme; free-phone service for tenants for emergencies	1990-	Local authority estates	22	Supplements on council tenants' rents	Local authority	No
11. Collingwood Housing Neighbourhood Wardens, Manchester	Crime prevention; environmental improvement On-site	management	No information	Housing association developments	3	Housing association	Housing association	Pending
12. Dacorum Borough Wardens	Environmental improvement	Patrol	1995-	Borough	No information	Local authority	Local authority	No
13. Dormanstown West Estate – 'Caretaking Plus', Cleveland	Environmental improvement	Appointment of Liaison Officer – for caretaking and on-site management	Pilot project 1995/6. New funding secured	Local authority estate – 220 tenanted houses, 22 owner occupied	1	Local authority	Local authority – assisted by PEP	Yes
14. Dundee City Council – security initiative plus Families Project	Crime prevention; environmental improvement; community development	Concierge scheme; security patrol; 'Families Project' (works with 'problem' families)	No information	Local authority estates across Dundee	No information	Local authority	Local authority	No
15. The Eldonian Community Warden Scheme, Liverpool	Crime prevention	Security patrol employed from long-term unemployed; victim services.	Pending	Eldonian and Athol Villages, Liverpool	8	Employment zone; Housing Corporation; Safer Merseyside Partnership; NIP	Eldonian Development Trust (community organisation)	Evaluation planned

APPENDIX A: OVERVIEW OF THE SCHEMES (continued)

Scheme	Functions	Methods	Duration	Area covered	No. of staff	Funding	Management	Evaluation/ monitoring
16. Exeter Community Patrol Service	Crime prevention	Uniformed patrol to act as the council's 'eyes and ears' outside office hours	1995-	Residential housing area and public places	8	Local authority	Local authority	No
17. Gipsyville Estate Warden Scheme, Hull	Environmental improvement	Caretaker; 'New Deal' initiative; on-site management	1998-	Local authority estate	6	SRB; local authority; New Deal	Hull Local Purchasing Initiative – (HLPI)	Evaluation planned
18. Glasgow City Centre Representatives	Crime prevention; environmental improvement	Uniformed patrols; provide information to public; liaise with public services; appointed from long-term unemployed	1995-	City Centre	44	Glasgow Works Programme (primarily)	Private security co. and partnership	Yes
19. Halifax Estate Officer	Environmental improvement	Supercaretaker role; focus on estate repairs and on-site management. Involves close contact with residents	1998-	Covers 150 units over three housing association estates	1	Housing association	Housing association	No
20. Hartlepool Central Estate project	Crime prevention; environmental improvement; community development	Active residents' association works in partnership with police and local authority; community worker appointed; on-site management	1994-	Local authority estate – approximately 600 dwellings	1	SRB; local authority	Partnership	CRA have completed an informal evaluation, surveys and projects
21. Headrow Liaison Tenants, Leeds	Environmental improvement	Liaison tenants appointed to attend to emergencies, repairs, and act as 'good neighbours'	1985-	Housing association developments of various sizes (up to 72 properties)	1 per development	Service charge	Housing association	No
22. Hemel Hempstead Town Centre Wardens	Crime prevention; environmental improvement	Patrol – appointed from long-term unemployed	1998-	Town centre	3	Part of local authority bid for European funding for an Immediate Labour Market	Project (ILM) Local authority	No
23. HOME Housing Association Resident Caretakers/ Estate Workers, Gateshead	Environmental improvement	Resident caretakers; liaison with tenants and appropriate agencies; on-site management	No information	Several housing association estates varying in size from 100-700 units	No information	Service charge and HOME Housing Association Payroll Budget	Housing association	No

APPENDIX A: OVERVIEW OF THE SCHEMES (continued)

Scheme	Functions	Methods	Duration	Area covered	No. of staff	Funding	Management	Evaluation/ monitoring
24. Horton Housing Association Community Support Agency, Bradford	Community development	Partnership approach to helping vulnerable people, e.g. 'Floating Support', 'Care Programme Approach Clients', 'Reachout', 'Community Integration Initiative' – includes employment and training services.	–	Local authority and housing association developments across Bradford	11	Housing Corporation SHMG; Dept. of Health; Charities, Housing Association	Partnership	Some monitoring of certain schemes
25. Hyndburn Borough Community Wardens Scheme, Lancashire	Crime prevention	High profile foot patrol; liaison with police	1995-8	Town centre	No information	Local authority; SRB; private sector	Private company	No
26. Kemsley Village – Caretaking Plus Scheme, Kent	Environmental improvement	Appointment of five staff for caretaking, on-site management and to tackle anti-social behaviour	1995-	Housing association estate	5	Local authority	Swale Housing Association	Yes
27. Kingsmead 'Community Trust', Hackney	Crime prevention; environmental improvement; community development	Use of conditions of tenancy to enforce standards of behaviour; organisation of community activities; partnership of local organisations	1992-	Local authority estate of 1,084 dwellings	No information	Local authority	Local authority	Yes
28. HOPE Halton Moor and Osmondthorpe Project for Elders, Leeds	Community development	Supports elderly people e.g. by fitting smoke alarms, providing gardening services, organising events	1995-	370 clients across 3 local authority estates	1	Local authority	Local authority; back-up provided by Anchor Trust	No
29. Lavender Croft Responsible Tenant, West Yorkshire	Environmental improvement	Provides out-of-hours presence; point of contact; reports anti-social behaviour; liaises with housing association; ensures properties are managed and maintained	1998	22 one bed flats for young single people	1	Housing association	Housing association	No
30. Leeds Federated Housing Association Resident Estate Worker	Environmental improvement	Resident caretaker; maintains properties; liaises with housing office	1994-	Housing association estate – 125 dwellings	1	Housing association	Housing association	No

APPENDIX A: OVERVIEW OF THE SCHEMES (continued)

Scheme	Functions	Methods	Duration	Area covered	No. of staff	Funding	Management	Evaluation/monitoring
31. Manningham Housing Association Mutual Aid Housing Compact, Bradford	Crime prevention; community development;	Selection of tenants with the view of creating an environment which discourages anti-social behaviour.	1998-	Housing association development of 25 dwellings	None	Housing association	Housing association	No
32. Middlesborough Council, Estate Caretaker Service	Crime prevention; environmental improvement	On-site caretakers; concierges in high rise blocks	1992-	Local authority estates across Middlesbrough	No information	B & N Housing Association	Housing association	No
33. Mitchelhill, Glasgow	Crime prevention; environmental improvement	Concierges; on-site management; extended tenant participation; partnership with police	1988-	Local authority estate	No information	Local authority	Local authority	Yes
34. Newport Borough Council Estate Ranger Service	Crime prevention; environmental improvement	Uniformed patrol – rapid response to anti-social behaviour	1994-	Local authority estates across Newport	15	Local authority	Local authority	Yes
35. North British Housing Association Estate Officers	Environmental improvement	Caretaking; liaison with housing officers	No information	Housing association developments in the North West	No information	Housing association	Housing association	No
36. Pepys Estate Resident Caretakers, Lewisham	Crime prevention; environmental improvement; community development	Resident caretakers; partnership with police; expansion of community associations	1982-	Local authority estate	12 resident caretakers	Local authority	Local authority	Yes
37. Possil Park Community Business, Glasgow	Crime prevention; environmental improvement; community development	Security patrols. Cooperative set-up by local unemployed people to improve security and environment	1986-	Local authority estate	No information	Early development funding from Strathclyde Community Business; self-sufficient after 4 years	Residents and local authority	Yes
38. The Raffles Estate, Carlisle, Tenant Support Workers	Crime prevention; environmental improvement	Concierges; support workers; formal links with police	1996-	Housing association estate	No information	Service charges, SHMG	Housing association	No

APPENDIX A: OVERVIEW OF THE SCHEMES (continued)

Scheme	Functions	Methods	Duration	Area covered	No. of staff	Funding	Management	Evaluation/monitoring
39. The Stadswacht (City Guard) Schemes, Netherlands	Crime prevention	Uniformed security patrols appointed from long-term unemployed	1994-	Cities and towns across the Netherlands	700	Central government; local authorities	Local authorities	Yes
40. Sedgefield Community Force	Crime prevention	Uniformed security patrol	1994-	Borough – 54 square miles	11	Local authority	Local authority	Yes
41. St. Edmundsbury Borough Council Community Ranger Service	Crime prevention; environmental improvement	Patrol	1998-	Borough – 34,000 households	No information	Local authority	Local authority	Pending
42. Stockport Town Wardens	Crime prevention	Security patrol; provides information to public; liaise with local authority; recruited from long term unemployed	1998-	Town	16	Local authority, SRB, European Social Fund	Local authority	Pending
43. Swansea Estate Warden and Neighbourhood Support Unit	Crime prevention; environmental improvement; community development	Patrols; witness support; CCTV; on-site management	1994-	Estates	The NSU employs 30 staff members	Local authority	Local authority	Yes
44. Sussex – 1066 Housing Association Tenant Caretakers	Environmental improvement	Caretakers	1997-	Housing association estates – 4,600 residents	No information	Housing association; tenant charge	No information	No information
45. Wandsworth Parks Police	Crime prevention	Uniformed patrols – zero tolerance; support for Metropolitan Police Service	1985-	4 Parks	37	Local authority	Local authority	Yes
46. West Mercia Parish Wardens Scheme	Crime prevention; environmental improvement	Provide two-way liaison between residents and police; visit the elderly	1993-	690 parishes, 400,000 mixed homes	8	Volunteers	West Mercia Police Force	Yes
47. Wessex Gardens Estate, Westminster	Crime prevention	Uniformed patrol – links with police	1993-	Local authority estate	No information	Rent and service charges	Local authority	No
48. West Yorkshire Housing Association Warden Scheme	Environmental improvement	Wardens liaise with tenants and housing association – on-site management role.	No information	Housing association estates	No information	Housing association	Housing association	Report

APPENDIX A: OVERVIEW OF THE SCHEMES (continued)

Scheme	Functions	Methods	Duration	Area covered	No. of staff	Funding	Management	Evaluation/monitoring
49. Wirral Community Patrol	Crime prevention	Uniformed patrol works in partnership with the police	1996-	Borough	32 Patrol officers; 8 supervisors; 16 control room officers	Local authority	Local authority	Some monitoring
50. Yorkshire Metropolitan Housing Association Estate Caretaker	Environmental improvement	Caretaker and on-site management	1996-	Housing association estate	No information	Housing association	Housing association	No

Appendix B: 'Working the Beat' – Fundamental Prinicples

Establishment of Schemes

Schemes should be established based on a locally expressed need which will allow for them to be tailored to that local need.

Powers

There should be no diminution of the powers of police officers. In respect of neighbourhood wardens and similar schemes, there should be no enhancement of powers beyond that of the ordinary citizen.

Intervention

The police must remain the only body with powers to intervene in situations without consent.

Other persons may only intervene with consent or under whatever arrangement lies between the employer of the warden/patrol and the citizen.

Government

Local authority patrols must be accountable to local authorities but, since their employment should arise from the community safety proposals of the Crime and Disorder Act, partnership working with the police is essential. However, they must bear responsibility for their own actions in joint initiatives whether with the police or other agencies.

Regulation

Regulation of the security industry must be vigorously pursued; in the interim the police should seek an active role in such matters as vetting and quality control to ensure that schemes are operating to an agreed acceptable standard.

Appearance

The appearance of non-police warden and patrol personnel must be distinct from that of the police in terms of uniform, livery and corporate image.

Standard Operating Procedures

Specimen standard operating procedures should be developed for a range of different locations (residential, town-centre), circumstances (intervention, patrol), relationship (local authority, private security) and purposes (information exchange, call responses). This must include reference to such matters as recruitment, training, managing processes and facilities management.

Funding

Complementary patrols and neighbourhood warden schemes should be funded from identifiable sources which do not involve any diminution of police budgets.

Related RDS Publications

Police Research Series papers

103. **Applying Economic Evaluation to Policing Activity.** J.E. Stockdale, C.M.E. Whitehead and P.J.Gresham. 1999.

108. **Preventing Residential Burglary in Cambridge: From crime audits to targeted strategies.** Trevor Bennett and Linda Durie. 1999.

Crime Detection and Prevention Series papers

60. **Policing and Neighbourhood Watch: Strategic issues.** Gloria Laycock and Nick Tilley. 1995.

65. **Local Crime Analysis.** Tim Read and Dick Oldfield. 1995.

74. **Policing Problem Housing Estates.** Sheridan Morris. 1996.

85. **Getting the Grease to the Squeak: Research lessons for crime prevention.** Michael Hough and Nick Tilley. 1998.

91. **Auditing Crime and Disorder: Guidance for local partnerships.** Michael Hough and Nick Tilley. 1998.

Policing & Reducing Crime Unit
Research, Development & Statistics Directorate
Home Office
Clive House, London SW1H 9HD

Tel: 020 7271 8225 Fax: 020 7271 8344

www.homeoffice.gov.uk/prghome.htm